Simple Works

Simple Ideas to Make Life Better

BLACK PANTS
PUBLISHING

Also by Chris Crouch
The Contented Achiever: How to Get What You Want and Love What You Get

Also by Susan Drake
The Practical Guide to Finance and Accounting,
The Pocket Idiot's Guide to the Portable Office and
Freelancing for Dummies.

Simple Works

Simple Ideas to Make Life Better

Presented to

_____

On this_____day of_____

_____

_____

_____

_____

_____

_____

By _____

Simple Works

Simple Ideas to Make Life Better

Chris Crouch Susan Drake

BLACK PANTS
PUBLISHING

To contact the authors with comments or to inquire about
speaking, seminars, or consulting, write to them at:

CCSeagull888@aol.com
sdrake@midsouth.rr.com

Published by Black Pants Publishing, LLC
3410 S. Tournament Drive
Memphis, TN 38125

Typography: Colleen Wells
Cover Design: Lightbourne

Publisher's Cataloging-in-Publication
(Provided by Quality Books, Inc.)

Crouch, Chris
     Simple works : simple ideas to make life better /
Chris Crouch, Susan Drake. -- 1st ed.
     p. cm.
     LCCN 2001089092
     ISBN 0-9703736-2-7

     1. Success. 2. Satisfaction. 3. Self-actualization
(Psychology) 1. Drake, Susan M. II. Title.

BJ1611.2.C76 2001   158.1
                           QBI01-700411

This book is printed on acid-free paper.

We dedicate this book to our children and grandchildren David, Diana, Kathryn, Colleen, Gabriel and Faith. We wish them luck in discovering simple ideas to make life better much sooner than we did.

Table of Contents

The writer does the most who gives the reader the most knowledge and takes from him the least time.

Sydney Smith

Simple Works

Introduction

The amazing artist Pablo Picasso once recounted that when he was a child his mother had ambitions for him. "If you become a soldier, you'll be a general. If you become a monk, you'll end up as Pope. Instead I became a painter and wound up as Picasso."

When we began this little book, we had aspirations to become painters. We hoped to paint short, inspiring little pictures that could help people lead simpler, more balanced lives. In the process, we assumed that it might also help us.

Just as Picasso's work evolved, this book has taken on a life of its own. It has essentially written itself, filling up with ideas we believe to be truths of a small, yet powerful nature.

It doesn't take a lot of effort to benefit from what's here. Just a bit of energy to try one or two of the ideas and to see if you feel you gain something of a happier existence. As you build one upon another, you may find that the results compound. Like a painting, this book has many layers, and as you add each layer it brings greater depth and dimension to the whole.

We believe the way to change lives is not a drastic, all-or-nothing event. It's a process of using simple tools and watching the amazing results grow and change. Pick one of these 26 short messages at random and try it. If you like what happens, try another. We are hoping this little book of simple messages can help you become a Picasso of your own life. Try it . . . it's a simple idea to make life better.

Aesthetic Arrest

"What have I done to deserve this experience?"

The best things in life are free; unfortunately, most of us get in such a hurry in life we forget to take advantage of the available supply of "free things." For me, art is one of those "free" things I want to continue to learn to appreciate. There was a time when I couldn't understand why and how some people got such pleasure going to museums and spending hours looking at what they considered great works of art. I admired people who had taken the time to learn about and appreciate art, but I was just not one of them. However, as they say, it's never too late to get started; so I decided to see what I could do to help me better understand and appreciate art.

Call it coincidence, luck, synchronicity, or whatever; within a short time after I decided to embark on my learning journey, a series of audiotapes called *Wings of Art* by Joseph Campbell mysteriously showed up in my life. While discussing the book *Portrait of an Artist* by James Joyce, Campbell talked about "proper art" and "improper art." He said proper art is static and *does not move you to do anything.* Improper art *moves you with desire, loathing or fear.* Strange, I've often heard of people being "moved" by great art; so I didn't understand why proper art would not move someone. Campbell explained that proper art puts the observer in a state of "aesthetic arrest," when, time stands still, distractions disappear, the mind becomes totally focused and the observer shifts into a maximum state of "noticing."

Campbell told a story about his astronaut friend, Russell Scheweickart, who was assigned an "extravehicular action" . . . a space walk. Russell's assignment required close coordination with another crewmember inside the shuttlecraft. Typically, every second of a space walk was perfectly choreographed, with little or no idle time. During this walk, however, there was some difficulty inside the shuttlecraft, and Russell was left outside with nothing to do for several minutes. He suddenly *noticed* his situation. He realized he was traveling 17,000 miles per hour through space . . . there was no wind and no sound. He looked in one direction and saw the moon. He looked in another direction and saw Earth. As he pondered his situation, he silently asked himself:

"What have I ever done to deserve this experience?"

At that moment, Campbell said, his friend was in *aesthetic arrest*. He was frozen in time. He was totally focused on the present experience, in a maximum state of *noticing*. He was unable to move, or to think about anything else. It was one of those rare moments of true bliss.

Maybe we can't all walk in space, travel 17,000 miles per hour and experience stunning views of celestial bodies; however, we can learn to *notice* some of the awesome "proper art" around us everyday. Some of the best things in life *are free* and all we need to do is un-ignore them.

After hearing Campbell's ideas about aesthetic arrest, I was surprised at how easy it was to *notice* beautiful and interesting things, and to have mini-aesthetic arrests. I realized part of the joy of life is paying more attention to the things that trigger the senses. I learned to stay in the present as I taste and touch things. To get more enjoyment from many of the various sights, sounds and smells that surround me each day. To enjoy the present bite of life more than spending my time thinking of the next bite. I learned that the sound of the train whistle blowing near our house doesn't have to be annoying; it can make me think of pleasant memories or intriguing journeys. I learned that I don't have to look much farther than a sunset in the summer, or a tree in the fall to experience aesthetic arrest. I learned experiences such as these *are* some of the best things in life and they *are* all free. I noticed I am (and have always been) surrounded by fascinating, interesting, beautiful things and people. I might not have learned much about art in an academic sense. I didn't learn much about artists and schools and techniques. But I did learn about the art that surrounds me everyday, and that I don't have to go to a museum to enjoy the stimulation of the senses that art can evoke. Sometimes all I have to do is be quiet, be still, look around and choose to view the world with a childlike sense of wonder and awe. It's such a joyful choice.

The best things in life are free. Look around, notice them, try it right now . . . it's a simple idea to make life better.

Balance

Some Extreme Thoughts on Balance

Have you ever seen little kids spin around and around until they get so dizzy they become totally out of balance and fall down? They try to get up a few times and fall down again and again. When they regain their equilibrium and their ability to stand up, what do they do? They start spinning around and around until they fall down again! Kids laugh and have a great time as they repeatedly spin around, lose their balance and fall. It's a fun game.

It's quite different with adults. With the exception of Grateful Dead fans and ice skaters, you don't see many "spinning adults" who seem to be having fun. *Fun* is a great indication that you are going in the right direction in life, and kids seem to be more of an authority on what is fun and what is not. That's why I pay close attention to kids when I'm trying to learn about a concept that will improve my life. So what do kids know about balance that we adults seem to have forgotten?

One of the most common recommendations offered in self-help and personal growth books and articles is to always "live a balanced life." In general, I think this is good advice; however, there is another side to every story, and balance is no exception.

First of all, in this complex and often uncontrollable world, it is very difficult and impractical to *always* maintain balance. Things happen that disrupt our plans. When we are temporarily out of balance we may begin to think, "Something is wrong with me." But periods in which we are out of balance may not only be good for us, they may also be necessary to assure a life of personal growth.

Kids don't get hung up on judging their "out-of-balance-ness;" they're not afraid of being temporarily unsteady and falling down. They seem to instinctively understand that learning, innovation, creativity and other activities that result in personal growth usually occur "at the edge of things," where you often risk temporarily losing your balance. High performance airplane drivers refer to this position as "the envelope." To improve their skills, they occasionally "push the envelope," going slightly beyond the edge of their current capabilities to a somewhat extreme position. They know it's probably not a good idea to stay out on the edge too long, or to go too far beyond their current edge; but they *learn from flirting with the edge.* And like kids, they actually call it "fun."

People who achieve great things in life are those who are willing to go to extremes to learn new things and stretch their current abilities. As they explore new possibilities, they often discover what once seemed like an extreme position eventually becomes normal. I know a shy person whose fear of making presentations was affecting her career possibilities. She finally screwed up enough courage to join Toastmasters, the public speaking group. In the beginning she considered the idea of speaking before a group to be an extreme concept, one with which she could never be comfortable. When she first tried it, she experienced heart palpitations, stomach queasiness and a faint feeling. But after a time "on the edge," she became more skilled, more confident, and eventually felt natural on stage. What was once an extreme idea, became normal. She could never have enjoyed this success if she hadn't been willing to go out on a limb and try something that at one point seemed extreme.

We can learn several things from kids, airplane drivers and my brave friend:

- Being *temporarily* out of balance is O.K.
- Personal growth is often a function of converting extreme positions to balanced positions.
- Everyone is internally wired (whether they know it or not) to seek personal growth. Going to the edge is where this growth can be found.
- Don't pay too much attention to books and gurus who suggest that you *always* should seek to live a balanced life. Occasionally go to the edge and grow.

The people at Apple computer, known for their passion for innovation, introduced a concept called "better sameness" in some of their advertising and promotional materials. Their belief is that if you never go to the edge of your current capabilities, all you can hope for in life is better sameness. And who wants that?

Balance your need for balance. Try occasionally going to *your* "edge" and enjoy the resulting growth. Pick an area of your life today and take this idea out for a spin. Don't be afraid or feel guilty about stumbling, falling down or being temporarily out of balance . . . it's a simple idea to make life better.

Certainty

In Order to Arrive at Certainty, You Must Travel Through Uncertainty

Have you ever heard a sad story about a couple who was going to take a dream trip together when they retired, and then death or illness cut short their long-awaited journey?

Or have you read about the sudden closing of a generations-old company, where thousands of loyal workers were thrown into shock, now uncertain about what they would do for the next 10 or 20 years?

Most of us crave certainty, want to know what to expect, and feel extremely uncomfortable when things are up in the air. Yet uncertainty is inevitable in life. When dramatic unexpected things happen, we become suddenly attuned to how tenuous our hold is on many things we hold dear. We want things to settle down, to go back to "normal" and to stabilize, and we try desperately to "get our arms around" things. We try to regain a sense of certainty.

Here's the true irony of the desire for certainty: The only way to be relatively certain of anything is to respond positively to the feeling of being uncertain. How do we do that? One way is to change our belief about uncertainty, and to look at it as an opportunity, rather than a threat. We can start thinking of uncertainty as an invitation to think.

Uncertainty is actually a catalyst that helps fuel our personal growth. If there were no uncertainty, some people would never be driven to learn new things. Perhaps you remember Archie Bunker, the lead character in the TV series *All in the Family*. Archie was a classic example of a person who was certain about almost everything in life. Week after week, Archie suffered frustration as the world rapidly changed around him and he tried to hold onto his beliefs about marriage, family, diversity, politics and life in general. Archie was so certain of everything that he had no catalyst for growth. No reason to question his beliefs. He didn't have any feelings of uncertainty to drive positive changes in his life. Like Archie, some people get stuck in life because *they can only believe what they already know.* They are afraid of finding out anything different.

If you allow uncertainty to provide the fuel for fear in your life, it will naturally result in excessive stress and will become a negative influence. However, you can let the same feeling of uncertainty result in curiosity; it can become a positive driving force to help you think, learn, grow and cope with otherwise difficult and stressful situations.

To effectively deal with uncertainty, you must be comfortable going from knowing (or thinking you know) something, to doubting your knowledge, and back to knowing again (often something different). In order to go from doubt to knowing something, you must develop a new belief or replace an old belief. Although this sounds simple, think about the process of developing a new belief. What happens between the moment you do not believe something until the moment that you do? What builds the bridge to allow you to crossover to the new belief? Normally you start seeking a new belief because you feel uncertain of something in your life. You challenge your knowledge, gather new facts, process new information and then make a decision to adopt a new belief. Hopefully, your new belief helps you understand the world a little bit better. And understanding the world better is what life is all about. Without the phase we call uncertainty, you will always be stuck in life . . . never able to move forward, grow and develop your full potential.

Learn to effectively deal with uncertainty by responding with curiosity instead of fear. When an unexpected or difficult situation arises, ask yourself, "What can I learn from this experience?" or "What change do I need to make as a result of this experience?" Then take action: Make a new choice or adopt a new belief that will take you in a positive direction.

The best path to certainty is to let go of the excessive need for it. Embrace uncertainty.

Respond to uncertainty with healthy curiosity. I've never run into a case where curiosity actually killed a cat. Let go of the excessive need for certainty, and deal effectively with the inevitable uncertainties that make up the journey called *your life* . . . a simple idea to make life better.

Dog or Cat?

The Not So Purr-fect Solution

Suppose you decide that you want a pet. You know exactly what you want: You want it to bark, wag its tail, get excited when it sees you and fetch sticks when you throw them across the yard. You've already decided to name your pet Fido. Since you are also a person of action, you immediately head to the pet store. Before the sun sets today, you are going to bring home a new pet. There is no need to fool around once you have made a decision . . . take action.

As you enter the pet store, the owner greets you and you quickly let her know that you want a barking, tail-wagging, stick-fetching pet. The owner seems hesitant. "Are you sure you wouldn't be interested in a fluffy, quiet, meowing pet that would fetch a ball of yarn?" she asks. "Absolutely not," you reply. "I know what I want and I think it should be obvious to you that I want a dog and I want one right now!" "Well, then," the owner replies, "we have a small problem. We don't have any dogs right now. We expect to have some soon, and I'll be happy to call you when we get them. Of course, if you're flexible you could consider a cat. We have a large selection of cats and we could offer you a very good deal. It may take some training, but maybe you could teach one of these cats to bark, wag its tail and fetch sticks. Most people think cats are very smart animals and you seem to be the kind of person who is very good at getting people or pets to do what you want."

"You make a very good point. I see no reason why I can't get a cat and teach it how to be a dog. Give me the cat and I'll train it." As the storeowner writes up the sale, she asks, "What are you going to call your pet?" "Fido," you say.

How do you think Fido's training is going to go? What are the odds that Fido will bark, wag his tail and fetch sticks? This may seem a very peculiar story, but similar dramas are played out over and over every day by otherwise perfectly normal human beings.

This simple idea to make life better comes from don Miguel Ruiz's book titled *Mastery of Love*. It's a simple but powerful analogy that can help all of us avoid a lot of stress in our lives. Paraphrasing his concept:

Don't get a cat and expect it to act like a dog!

Most of us wouldn't think of doing this with a pet, but for some reason we think this theory will work perfectly well on humans. We know, for example, that our spouses or friends or coworkers have certain habits, characteristics, or traits that define them, and they may be traits that we don't really like. Rather than accepting people as they are and "allowing" them to be what they are, we react in one of several unproductive ways. For example, we:

- Secretly decide we will change them over time and correct the obvious flaws that are inconsistent with our image of "how they should be."
- Decide not-so-secretly we will change them, and embark on an all-out campaign to eliminate their flaws. Nagging is usually the main weapon in this battle of good (what we believe) over evil (what they believe).
- Threaten to do something unpleasant to them if they don't change.
- Threaten to do something undesirable to ourselves if they don't change.

In effect, we clearly see we have a cat on our hands and we decide we are going to change it into a dog. Here's our advice on this strategy:

It won't work!
Give it up!
Cats don't bark!
Cats don't fetch sticks!
Cats don't wag their tails!
Cats don't necessarily get
excited when they see you!

You only have the possibility to control half of any relationship with another human being. Therefore, better choices would be to:

- Unconditionally accept the person as they are and focus on points of harmony in your relationship.
- Change something about yourself. Usually the "evil" you observe in others is high on your mind because you practice the behavior yourself. As some people say, "If you spot it, you've got it."
- If possible, eliminate or minimize your interaction with the person. When you can't accept a person as they are, and you feel constant turmoil over it, you may need to find a situation more in keeping with your beliefs and needs.

Think of all the time and energy you will have if you quit trying to change others from "cats" into "dogs." You may even have the time and energy to have two pets . . . a dog and a cat. Thank you don Miguel Ruiz . . . you have given us a simple idea that will make life better.

Emotions

Thinking About Your Feelings

What should you do with all those messy emotions that keep popping up all over the place?

Some people believe you should avoid emotions, and certainly *never* let your emotions be your guide. They think you should be totally rational, hiding your feelings and always letting logic dictate your actions. Others believe (or feel) you should *always* let your emotions be your guide. "Go with your gut," they advise.

As a general rule, statements are incorrect if they include the words "never" or "always." The exception to this general rule is that there is *never* one right answer to a question and there are *always* several acceptable answers to a particular question. Therefore, let's look at the two sides of this coin called emotions and see if we can make heads or tails of this issue.

First, let's simplify the topic of emotions. There are really only two types of emotions: emotions that make you *feel good* and emotions that make you *feel bad*. They may be called by many names such as happiness, joy, fulfillment, comfort, sadness, anger, frustration, fear and others; however, they all fall into one of these two categories, feeling good and feeling bad.

Feeling good and feeling bad can both serve as excellent internal guides to help you make decisions about the direction you should consider taking in life. On the surface, it would seem logical to steer toward things that make you feel good and try to avoid things that make you feel bad.

But the important thing to remember about emotions, whether they make you feel good or bad, is that *they are trying to tell you something*. Emotions are like a wake-up call. They say, "Good morning. There's something significant going on here that you should probably take a closer look at."

Emotions that make you feel bad may not actually be

bad. Strong emotions may simply be an early warning sign that you are changing, or that you need to make a change. They may be the normal result, for example, of getting out of your comfort zone. That's why it is important to be aware of them, acknowledge them and examine them. If whatever is on the other side of the comfort zone is something you desire, it may just be a matter of understanding that this is part of the process of learning and growing. In this case, these temporary emotions that are making you feel bad are actually taking you in a direction that will eventually make you feel good. It is sort of like trying to explain to a sick child why they need to go to the doctor and get a shot. The shot will hurt now, but it will make you feel better in the near future. Understanding this can help you deal with and not overreact to emotions that generate negative feelings.

On the other hand, if your emotions generate good feelings, you also need to examine what they are telling you. They could be reinforcement that you're headed in the right direction. There is also a possibility that what feels good for *you* may be inappropriate when you consider others. For example, you may feel good when you drive fast. That's fine if you are a professional racecar driver in a properly equipped vehicle on a track at Daytona, but it is inappropriate if you are driving through a school zone when children are present.

Should you allow your emotions to guide you? You really have little choice, because while logic helps you get to the edge of a decision, emotions take you over the edge and almost certainly drive your final choice. Think about some of the major life decisions most people make such as getting married, buying a house, or a car, or deciding on a career.

Learn to learn from your emotions. Be sensitive to them and aware of what they are trying to tell you. Don't overreact to emotions that make you feel bad; they may just be a normal part of growing out of your comfort zone. If the bad feelings persist and you cannot understand how they are leading you to a better life, it might be time to make a change or ask for help.

Emotions that feel good and emotions that feel bad are both beneficial. Nurture them and be thankful for these inner guides that are telling you when you're on the right track in life . . . it's a simple idea to make life better.

Forgiveness

Who's on the Receiving End?

Reading is one of my true passions. On rare occasions my eyes will pass over words in a book and they will be like a neon sign. They make such perfect sense that the words, thoughts and concept will be immediately burned into my memory and join my core beliefs. That is exactly what happened to me one day when I was reading a book called *In the Spirit of Business* by Robert Roskind. What I read has stuck with me from the second I read it to this day. Chapter One, page 10:

"Resentment does more damage to the vessel in which it is stored, than to the object on which it is poured."

When I read that comment, it was like an epiphany. At that instant I adopted a core belief about the concept of forgiveness.

To me, the quote from Roskind's book says about all you really need to say about forgiveness. These twenty-one words hold the secret to much of what holds back the growth and development of the human race: We focus too much time and energy on the "guilty" person, holding onto resentment and what we believe to be "justified anger," instead of realizing what the state of unforgiveness does to us.

I've always heard that forgiving is a good thing to do *for the "guilty" person.* There are two problems with this approach:

1. The "guilty" person may not know or think they need our forgiveness. How can you be doing something nice for them when they don't know or care about the nice thing you're doing?

2. The "forgiving" person is the one who is actually suffering to begin with. Think about how you feel when you are angry or resentful of someone. Can't you physically feel the stress, the knot in your stomach, the neck pain, the headache, the tenseness of your muscles? And what about your

mental state? Are you ruminating about the situation and what the other person owes you? How much of your time are you investing in thinking of the situation? So, who is suffering from your unforgiving nature or attitude? *You are!* My conclusion: Practice forgiveness for your <u>own</u> good!

You may never be able to forget a real or perceived transgression, but you must learn to move on, forgive others and let the negativity go. Is it easy? At first it may seem almost impossible, especially if you feel your anger is justified. What was done to you may have been real and very, very wrong, but what has happened has happened and that is that. With practice you can learn to release the intangible negative energy and begin your healing process.

Let go of resentment, empty your vessel of anger or hurt, and make room for healing. It will allow you to free up your energy, find the time to do the things you love, and make room for more joy to enter your life. Try it right now. Pick a family member, co-worker or in some cases a stranger who is the target of your resentment. Let the resentment go and think about who benefits the most from your choice . . . it's a simple idea to make life better.

Guilty of Being Guilty

Yes, Your Honor, Human as Charged

As a good little self-help and personal growth book writer, I am supposed to tell you that you must let go of guilt, . . . and that there is absolutely no value in feeling guilty about anything. That's what I am supposed to tell you. Nah!

In the real world, most people cannot avoid feeling guilty at times. Some people actually choose to spend some of their time *feeling guilty about feeling guilty.* Guilt is almost a national pastime. Admittedly, there may be some people in the world who have gotten beyond any feelings of guilt. However, they do not need to read this book. I need to read their book. As a matter of fact, I feel a little guilty that I haven't already read it.

Let's assume if you are a member of the human race who is reading (or writing) this book that you occasionally feel guilty about something. What can we learn about guilt that will help us deal with it in a productive manner?

First, get in the habit of dividing guilt into two categories . . . guilt over something you *can do* something about and guilt over something you *can't do* anything about.

Start with guilt over something that you can do something about, like the way you feel if you hurt someone's feelings, tell a lie or slack off at work. You know you can and should make amends or change your behavior.

Most of the time, this type of guilt fits into either the "I *shouldn't* have done that" guilt category, or the "I *should* have done that" guilt. The best solution to this type of guilt is:

1. *Quit* doing what you shouldn't be doing, or
2. *Start* doing what you should be doing, and then
3. *Move on!*

You're going to feel guilty from time to time, so why not use your guilt feelings as a call to action and a trigger for change? Allow guilt to be your teacher instead of your tormentor.

Then, there's the second type of guilt: guilt you can't do anything about. This might include feeling guilty because you dropped the winning touchdown pass twenty years ago, or that you had an argument with someone right before they died. In both these cases, the event is over and done. You can't change it now. Go immediately to step 3: move on!

Don't waste too much time feeling guilty about guilty feelings. If your guilt is the kind of guilt most of us wrestle with everyday, you are probably just guilty of being human. Find out what your guilty feelings are trying to teach you, learn the lesson, respond and move on with life . . . it's a simple idea to make life better.

Happiness

Tornadoes, Floods and Wars of Joy

The Storm

It was April 1977, the force of the storm was awesome, the devastation was appalling. Everything in the path of the powerful, twisting funnel of wind was almost completely destroyed. In the aftermath of the violence, the people of the community worked together to pick up the pieces of their lives. Within a few short days, they mourned and buried the dead, cared for the injured, cleared the debris and began rebuilding their homes and businesses. Petty differences were temporarily unimportant. Social status was temporarily unimportant. Racial, political and religious differences were temporarily unimportant . . . for a few short days, only *working together* to rebuild their lives was important. As time passed and the physical wounds of the storm healed, many people in the community looked back on April 1977 as their *"finest moment."*

The Flood

The whole town turned out to pitch in and help. Some people filled bags with sand; others quickly put the bags in place. It was inevitable that the levee was going to break if they could not stop the flow. It was amazing how such a life-giving force could turn on them so quickly. The rain so desperately needed just a few weeks ago was now threatening to destroy their community. A few of the older citizens remembered the last time the levee broke over 40 years ago. They remembered the almost unimaginable destruction and the long painful road to recovery. They must stop the flow. Every mind, every heart, and every body in the community was totally focused on *working together* to stop the flow. After days of intense activity, worry, anxiety and prayer, the water finally subsided. Together, they had stopped the flow. They felt fortunate, they felt relieved, they felt the joy of the spirit of cooperation, they felt it was their *"finest moment."* And with the passage of time, they wondered why they had such fond memories of such tragic times.

The War

The old soldier knelt on the ground beside the grave of his best friend who did not survive the battle. His friend and all the other members of his platoon were dead. All those who had worked together to defeat the common enemy now lay silent. As the last remaining survivor, it was up to him to solve the mystery. He didn't think he would be around much longer so he needed to solve it soon. During the battle, he had never been so scared in his life. Why did nations have to settle things with war? Why did young men have to fight the wars of old men? Why did ordinary people have to fight the wars of politicians? But his real fight now was to simply explain the unexplainable. He would soon join the others who fought so bravely on that day in 1944; but he *had to understand it* before he died. The battle had occurred over fifty years ago and he still didn't understand why in the midst of all the horror and chaos of war *he found such joy*. Life had been so easy since the war had ended. He didn't understand why after surviving the war and living over fifty years in peace and prosperity, he looked back on his time in combat as his *"finest moment."* Why did he have such fond memories of such tragic times?

The Connection

What do these three stories have in common? In each case the circumstances were tragic and often terrifying. In each case the people had little time to focus on the day-to-day problems, issues and concerns that often consume our time and energy. And with the passage of time, something unusual happened to many of the people involved in the events. Rather than remembering only the tragic circumstances of the ordeal, they also had deep-felt, *positive feelings* about being a part of a group of people who worked together to overcome adversity. Over time, the tragic events had actually become a source of pleasure for them and were remembered as one of the finest moments of their life. One definition of joy is "a feeling of great pleasure or happiness, or a source of pleasure." What was it about tragedy that made it a source of joy and happiness? What can we learn from this observation?

We can learn that happiness is not only about smiling, laughing and easy times. Happiness is also about:

- Being a part of something that is greater than yourself and your personal needs.
- Being committed to something that is clearly an important, meaningful mission.
- Being a part of a group that disregards the status and labels often dictated by society.
- Being fully engaged in the moment, giving the task at hand 100% of your time and attention.
- Being able to transcend you current circumstances and find joy even as you face tragedy.

It's easy to be happy when all is right with your world. But the world sometimes kicks you around, beats you up and gives you a hard time. It is almost as if the world is testing you to "see what you are made of." Every time the world kicks you, you once again have the opportunity to make a choice. You can choose to go into a downward spiral and let the situation get the best of you; or, you can choose to transcend the circumstances and possibly turn it into one of your finest moments.

Happiness and joy are not just about having fun. Happiness is about fully experiencing life, good and bad. Regardless of the circumstances you are in right now, choose happiness . . . it's a simple idea to make life better.

Inspiring People

The Ultimate Motivational Technique

Over the years, I have read many books and heard many speakers talk on the topic of motivation. Sometimes the more you read and the more you hear about motivation, the more confusing it becomes. Based on my unofficial, un-qualified and unencumbered by professional credentials research on the topic, here are some of my conclusions about motivation.

Most people, maybe even all people, seem to be motivated by one of two emotions . . . fear or desire. But what exactly is it they fear or desire? It seems to be related to one of six things:

1. Fear related to lack of control over some aspect of
   their life
2. Fear related to lack of security
3. Fear related to lack of approval from others
4. Desire for control over some aspect of their life
5. Desire for security
6. Desire for the approval of others

Maybe there are more broad categories related to fears
and desires; I don't know, but these six cover a lot of
ground. They are a good starting point for discovering
how to understand what makes people tick.

Advertising executives and sales people are notorious
for using these six ideas when they are trying to help
people make buying decisions. "If you will just use our
brand of automobile, you will enjoy the control and
freedom of the open road, you will be safe and secure
even if you decide to crash our product into a test lab
wall, and people will think you look marvelous and
successful." "If you will wear our clothes, people will
approve of you." "If you buy our insurance, you will
have security for life." "If you invest with us, you will
have control over your life." It goes on and on twenty-
four hours a day.

Maybe we can learn from these advertising and sales
people. We may not sell products directly, but all of us
must sell something everyday. We must persuade our

spouse, boss, customer, children or someone else of something . . . and that is selling. If we understand the six broad categories of fears and desires, we have two choices as to how we'll go about persuading others. *We can scare them or inspire them.* I think both techniques, if applied skillfully, will result in success. Playing on people's fears works. It is a proven method. But why not use the same amount of effort to inspire people. As a salesperson, parent, spouse or friend, ask questions and listen. Find out what is really important to others and help them develop a plan of action that will inspire them to achieve their goals. You will end up at the same place but the journey will be much more enjoyable for you and your "customer."

Say and do inspiring things that help others with their quest to gain control over their lives, remain secure and enjoy a reasonable amount of approval from others. Think of the times someone has truly inspired you. How did it feel? Try to pass it on and make someone in your life feel that way today . . . it's a simple idea to make life better.

Judging

Half Full, Half Empty, or Just a Glass of Water

There are two easy ways to meet people:

- Get pregnant, or
- Go on a diet.

These are foolproof methods of attracting absolute strangers to discuss the most intimate details of their experience with both situations. (In the case of pregnancy, they will even feel completely justified putting their hand on your belly, as if your belly is not a part of your personal anatomy.) They will, in fact, feel compelled to tell you everything they know about these subjects, including all the latest medical findings, true life horror stories, and the amazing thing that happened to their Aunt Lorraine. Surprisingly, they don't need to know anything about your situation to give you advice. You could be diabetic, having twins, recovering from anorexia or have a myriad of other health factors that would be important to your condition. But to armchair doctors, none of it matters. They can size up your situation and develop a treatment plan without facts. Of course, they probably won't be around for the outcome, so their accuracy doesn't exactly matter.

It sounds pretty presumptuous, doesn't it? But I suspect we all do it sometimes, either to ourselves or to others. Think about it: Have you ever jumped to a conclusion about your own life situation without all the information you need? I'll bet you have. Here's a little test. Pretend you've just found out that you've been fired from your job. What's your immediate reaction to that thought? If you're like most people, it will be, "Oh, this is the worst thing that could happen." You're looking at the situation in the "micro," and deciding that it's a bad thing. But you've made that judgment with only a tiny shred of information.

Now imagine what your life *could be like* six months from now. Here's what might actually happen. Having lost your job you're forced to update your resume. As you revise it, you realize that you've done some pretty impressive things in your career. You're stung by the firing, but it gives you a chance to recount and feel good about your accomplishments. You decide, "Hey, I'm pretty darned good." You get on the Internet and discover some great job-finding resources, post your resume, and get an interview in San Diego. Now you land a new job, making more money, in a city you like. Tomorrow, you might even meet the woman or guy of your dreams. Was getting fired a bad thing? Consider what could have happened if you hadn't been fired. You'd still be in the current job, but you would miss out on all that other *wonderful* stuff that could happen. (In fact, studies show that the overwhelming majority of people who are fired get better, higher paying jobs than the ones they were fired from! Yet we all consider being fired to be a "bad" thing.)

Judging the things that happen to us is pretty much a waste of time, because we can't possibly see far enough down the road to tell what the results will be. More and more, I try to accept situations as they are, without deciding they're good or bad. Until I can see the whole picture, there is no way I can see where I'm headed, or just what paths will take me there.

Okay, we looked at how something that looks bad can actually lead to something that seems good. Now let's take a reverse example. When Sharon Christa

McAuliffe was selected as the first high school teacher to take a ride on the Challenger space shuttle, many people thought that was the most wonderful thing that could happen. No doubt there were celebration parties, congratulatory notes and smiles all around. At the time of the announcement, it seemed a fabulous thing. But sadly, the spacecraft exploded just seconds after takeoff, and Christa's family lost her forever. Was her participation in that mission a good thing, or a bad one? From the short perspective at the time of her selection it might be good; later, it might be considered bad. Still later, when you consider the children who might have been inspired by her story, or the changes to the spacecraft that might prevent future tragedies, or the many other possible positive results, it's impossible to put a judgment on the event. As strange as it may seem at times, there is no real value in judging an event as either positive or negative in the short run.

What happens to us along our path, whether it's painful or joyful at the moment, can teach us about ourselves and our journey. In the moment, we can never determine what lesson we will ultimately learn from our current situation. In the moment, we can simply remember to remain open to the lessons offered as the events of our lives unfold. As we travel along the road of life, there will be many events. They won't be good events or bad events; they will simply be events. It's not helpful to judge them, because anytime we're judging, we're like the armchair doctor, diagnosing based on incomplete information. Not judging what happens in our lives . . . a simple idea to make life better.

Knowledge

What a Know-It-All

Years ago I attended a lecture by Dr. Edwards Deming, a management expert who is often credited with helping the Japanese make quantum leaps in the quality of their products and the overall health of their post-war economy. The lecture took place not long before Dr. Deming died. Although I think he was in his nineties, he impressed me as being very sharp, mentally alert and younger in spirit than most people a third his age.

Although his remarks were fascinating, I learned my most valuable lesson from the question and answer period at the end. After he had answered a few questions from the audience, one person asked a multi-part question that dragged on forever and seemed designed to back Dr. Deming in a corner. At the end of the question, the audience member said, "What do you think I should do?" Without the slightest hesitation, Dr. Deming stood up, looked him in the eye and said, "There is no substitute for profound knowledge," and sat down. Probably thinking that Dr. Deming "didn't get it" the antagonist rephrased the question. Once again, Dr. Deming stood up and said, "There is no substitute for profound knowledge," and sat down. After one more try and the same response from Dr. Deming, the audience member gave up. The audience member seemed totally frustrated with Dr. Deming, but Dr. Deming seemed very pleased with the exchange.

If you've spent much time in a classroom environment, you know that when a professor says something three times, you'd better pay attention. It usually means:

1. The professor is getting senile, or
2. This nugget is important and *it is going to be on the test!*

Dr. Deming was most definitely not senile; therefore, I surmised that what he said (three times) must have been important. At first I was stumped, but the more I thought about it the more I realized he was telling us not just the answer to the audience member's question but also the answer to almost any question. You see, one of Dr. Deming's specialties was ferreting out the solution to a problem others had missed by jumping to an erroneous conclusion. (One of his famous "discoveries," for example, is that bad people don't cause most manufacturing problems, bad processes do.)

How often do we shortcut our learning processes, trying to operate with only a surface knowledge of a topic or process? Think of it . . . how many of your current frustrations, fears and failures would disappear if you went beneath the surface and developed a more *profound knowledge* of what you're dealing with? Dr. Deming seemed to choose his words carefully, and even though I knew the meaning of "profound," I looked it up. American Heritage defines profound as "extending to or coming from a great depth." Often in life, I am a "throw away the instruction sheet and put the stupid thing together" person. I usually pay for my lack of profound knowledge by getting electrical shocks or having unexplained extra pieces at the completion of assembly. This approach invariably leads to frustration and often failure. Other times, I get fully engaged, dig in and develop a deep understanding of what I am doing. Taking the time to develop a deeper knowledge of whatever you are doing pays off in every area of your life. For example:

- Greater knowledge of your job could give you greater confidence and more career success.

- Greater knowledge of child psychology would help you raise healthier children.
- Greater knowledge of your personal strengths and weaknesses would help you build on the former and improve the latter.
- Greater knowledge of others and their needs would enhance your relationships.

The list is as infinite as the knowledge available on the planet.

The root cause of most all fears, frustrations and failures is a lack of sufficient knowledge. Profound knowledge mitigates fear, frustration and failure. Not only that, but profound knowledge results in the opposite . . . joy, fulfillment and success.

It is as simple as this, whatever you are facing, if you understand it better . . . you can better deal with it. Start simple. Find a small area of your life that is causing you frustration or fear and go on a personal quest to develop a better understanding of it. Then tackle a bigger issue, and another, and another using Dr. Deming's universal answer to all questions. "There is no substitute for profound knowledge" . . . it's a simple idea to make life better.

Letting Go

Flying Through the Air
With the Greatest of Ease

Trapeze artists who are first learning how to soar through the air begin by just swinging back and forth on one swing. As they become more comfortable with the height and feel of the swing, someone on the other side pushes an empty swing toward them, back and forth, back and forth. The trapeze trainees start to visualize letting go, seeing themselves flying through the air and grabbing the other swing. As with many things, thinking is easy, doing is hard. No matter how many times they swing back and forth, no matter how comfortable they are with this part of the process, no matter how much they think about letting go . . . actually letting go is tough. But one thing is clear . . . *if the trapeze artist never lets go, they will never get to the other side.* From the time they let go of one swing until they grab the other one they must deal with something we call fear. What ultimately gets trapeze artists from one side to the other is faith or trust. They have a confident belief they will make it to the other side.

You probably don't intend to become a trapeze artist, but you will inevitably be staring at that scary space "between the swings" many times throughout your life. Everyone approaches the edge where fear resides and they must make a choice. Will I let this fear keep me from moving forward or will I rely on faith and trust to get me to the "other side?"

I have made both choices in life. Some choices have stopped my growth, limited my freedom and stolen my joy. Other choices have taken me to new heights and allowed me to look back with curiosity about why I hesitated at the edge. Why did I wait so long to let go? At the same time I ask these questions, I often stand on the edge of the next cliff, hesitating to simply let go and trust that I cannot control everything about my life. In order to evolve, I must surrender to forces much more powerful than I who are *always* there for me and *always willing to help if I will only ask for help.* Courage is not about the lack of fear; courage is about being afraid and doing it anyway.

It might be nice if we could go through life always knowing what to expect next; always having hard evidence and tangible proof that we need not fear anything new we choose to try. Having tangible proof of what to expect next in life is great if you can get it. However, always relying on tangible proof to move forward in life will place severe limitations on the journey you are offered. Life constantly offers wonderful, magical and sometimes challenging uncertainty that when properly approached can offer rich, rewarding and growing experiences. Learning to let go and rely on faith and trust will open doors allowing you to go places and experience things that will never be available to those who have an unhealthy need for certainty.

The more you practice letting go and relying on trust and faith, the more you will understand it and be able to use its power. It's a simple idea I wish I had tried much sooner in my life. Letting go . . . it's a simple idea to make life better.

Miracles

Home Runs and Base Hits

Inspiration can come from some of the oddest places. I recently went to a major league baseball game and saw this quote: "Don't be swayed by flamboyance posing as innovation." It made me think about the flamboyant aspect of what we commonly refer to as "miracles."

Living in Memphis, Tennessee, home of St. Jude Children's Research Hospital, we get to hear about a lot of miracles when children are treated and recover from otherwise fatal illnesses. St. Jude is a cancer treatment facility, and people from all over the world come here seeking help. In fact, a friend of mine moved here because her 3-year-old son, Damien, was diagnosed with leukemia and was referred to St. Jude.

Damien is grown now. He's been in remission for a long, long time. I certainly consider that a miracle . . . a flamboyant one.

It's easy to focus on such bold, breathtaking events, and perhaps to wish that we could experience something like that in our lives. But what about all the tiny, subtle events that happen to us each day that are equally miraculous? They really are equally noteworthy.

Think about the discovery of penicillin. When the baker made the loaf of bread that eventually molded and yielded penicillin, no one recognized it as a miracle. The baker didn't say, "Well, I think I'll get up and create a wonder drug today." Nonetheless, the result of his ordinary work led to wonderful cures. And think about some of the miraculous things you can do everyday to change the world and make it a better place. You can write a note to someone or make a nurturing comment to them that may alter the course of their life. You can call a friend at just the moment they need to hear from you and help them through a rough spot in their life. You can create a memory for a child that will result in a lifetime of pleasant feelings and memories.

I have a friend who has told me time after time about a childhood experience that she will never forget. When my friend was young, her grandmother would invite her over for popcorn making adventures. Yes, I know people do not usually think of making popcorn as an adventure, but her grandmother was no ordinary popcorn maker. At the moment the kernels of corn began to pop, her grandmother would remove the lid and let the popcorn pop out onto the stove, and the counter, and the floor, and all over the kitchen. Nobody cared if you ate popcorn off the floor. Nobody cared about the mess it would make in the kitchen. Nobody cared what people would think of this peculiar behavior. Nobody cared about any of the popcorn making rules. This event was all about a miracle-making, popcorn-popping grandmother and her granddaughter. The grandmother lived a wonderful life and is long gone from this world. But her spirit and the miracles she created over thirty years ago still live on. The granddaughter is a mom now with her own young daughter. You guessed it. Her daughter and her small friends scream with delight when the popcorn flies out of the pan and into their memories. Miracles aren't hard to perform. Often it just takes a little caring and imagination.

Unless we see the true miracles of every day life, we may miss the most important part of the miracles.

Now, think about that inspirational baseball game I saw in Florida. Even that was a source of miracles. Do you doubt that? Think about this: When you see a player hit a home run, that's just the big finale. But it's all the practice and years of experience that combine to create a home run. As the batter stands at the plate, it's the miracle of his vision, his ability to move his muscles in unison, all the physical and mental interworkings that are the miracles that create the home run. The home run is just the manifestation of all those other factors.

Don't we have miracles in every single moment of our lives? Just the fact that we breathe in and out is a miracle. It's not flamboyant, but it is something pretty important to each of us.

If you look at your life as ordinary, and feel that nothing "miraculous" ever happens to you, think again. Our whole existence is a series of little miracles. Calling a friend and having them understand is a miracle. Being able to speak confidently to a client is a miracle. Watching your child at play is a miracle.

Seeing and appreciating the small miracles in your life . . . a simple idea to make life better.

Next Step

Taking the First Step in
the Right Direction

My daughter is a person I admire tremendously for a host of wonderful qualities. Among them are her courage and her insight. I was at her place recently, and she was in the middle of what for her was a normal day. Picture this: She was holding her 18-month-old daughter on her hip, filling a bottle for the baby and a sippy cup for her three-year-old son, calling a courier to pick up a delivery to take to her client (she's self-employed), and looking up the number for the utility company so she could get her lights, gas and water transferred before she moves to her new house.

That was just during one five-minute period. *Wow!* Remember that old joke about a parent telling the child, "I used to walk to school barefoot in the snow." Forget it. Nothing I did in my life could compare with how she juggles.

Most people—including me—would have found this situation overwhelming. I asked her, "How do you do it?" And she said, "I just keep thinking about taking one *next step.*"

Life has gotten so complicated. I think of a simple act like writing a letter. In the olden days, we used to write a letter, put it in an envelope, put a stamp on it, and mail it. By the time it arrived and someone responded, the turnaround time might be two or three weeks! Not anymore. In this day of electronic helpers—the computer, fax, email, voicemail, personal data assistants—we are pressured to do twelve things at a time, and to get them done faster and faster. Our to-do lists get longer, and our time to do them gets shorter, until it's easy to become swamped with everything we have to do.

Not only that, but we all have such big plans. We get our lives all planned out and our expectations of ourselves and others become monumental. It's not enough anymore to get up, eat breakfast, get dressed and go to work. We have to have big careers, big achievements, big vacations, big houses, big parties. How can we possibly get it all done?

The easy way, of course, would be to simplify our lives, to just do less. But even if we pare down what we must do, our magnifying minds can run rampant with the list of what we want to do.

It doesn't have to be that way if we concentrate only on *the one next step*. For example, as I sit at this computer, I don't have to write an entire book tonight. I don't even have to write a chapter. All I have to do this moment is finish this sentence! In fact, all I have to do at this moment is move my finger to type one letter at a time. Slowly but surely, if I finish one sentence at a time, the book will be written.

Break your activities down into manageable chunks and you can accomplish anything you want. If you've decided you want to go back to school, don't focus on how you're going to do the homework for your three classes (that you haven't even signed up for!). Focus on looking up the number in the phone book to call and get information about classes. Stay calm, and do *the one next step,* and things will miraculously get done.

It reminds me of when I've spilled dry pasta on a countertop. I get very impatient because it's hard to pick up dry pasta quickly. There's no way to scoop up handfuls. You have to clean it up a few noodles at a time, until you must pick up the last few pieces individually. In life, you also have to pick up the noodles one at a time.

Small steps add up to big advances. Taking things one step at a time . . . a simple idea to make life better.

One Right Answer

Pathfinders Paradise

Recently, my spouse and I had the opportunity to visit a very nice resort on an island in the Caribbean. The resort had many fine restaurants, pools, shops and other recreation areas. It also had a matrix of paths and sidewalks connecting the various facilities. We were vacationing with friends who had visited the resort before, so the first couple of days we just followed them around. I kept getting the sensation that I was going in circles (or actually more like squares). I also noticed that occasionally people walking behind us would take a different path and end up ahead of us. I certainly don't believe you have to walk the most efficient path all the time, especially when you're on vacation. Still, I was curious about why our friends consistently walked in the same circles and squares to get from point A to point B.

On our third day, everyone else went to the beach, and I stayed behind to read and do some writing. After a while, I decided to go exploring on my own. Sure enough, I discovered there were many different, and sometimes much shorter, ways to get from one facility to another. I found it odd that my friends hadn't followed these more convenient paths, but I just filed that away as an interesting facet of human behavior. I didn't plan to ever say anything about my discovery. I knew I'd suffer some ridicule if they learned I'd been playing the "Boy Scout Pathfinder."

The next day we were caught outside in a very heavy rain. As we were all trying to quickly take cover, my friends headed down the road that would lead us in circles and squares *in the rain.* Since I knew a much shorter (and therefore drier) way to get where we were going, I said to the group, "Let's go this way." Someone commented, "Oh, I didn't know you could get there this way," and they followed me and we all arrived at our destination much quicker and drier.

When you get caught in a "sudden rain," why not consider taking a different path than you might be accustomed to? Often, our usual, familiar way of dealing with things may seem more comfortable, but by following the same routine paths we may miss out on other good roads.

In my vacation trip, I saw there were many right paths. The scenery was different, the distance was different, but they all led to the same goal. In life, just like in my vacation, there is never just one right answer . . . never just one right path.

Taking a new path means getting out of your comfort zone, trying something unknown, taking a risk. But it can also allow you to have joyful, growth experiences. What can you do today to try out a new path? Maybe you can do something simple like buy a new CD and listen to a different kind of music or learn to cook a different meal. You could take piano lessons, buy a convertible, or fly in a hot air balloon. You could travel to an exotic place. You could find a way to make a living by using your true gifts and talents. Why not be open to new paths and different answers before the rain begins to fall too hard? Why not sit down right now and make up a list of 10 new things you are going to do before you are 30, 40, 50 or whatever age? There is not one right answer to how your life should unfold from this moment on. Why not be on the lookout for more than one right path or answer to the challenges of life?

Why not? Get a piece of paper and a pencil and make a list right now . . . it's a simple idea that can make life better.

Planning

Fluid Commitments and Frequent Adjustments

As the saying goes, "any virtue taken to an extreme can become a vice." Nowhere do I think this applies more than to the art or science (whichever you prefer) of planning. At one extreme you have people who never plan anything. They are worried that planning will inhibit their freedom of choice and spontaneity. On the other hand, you have people who plan everything down to the most minute detail of a project or event, and are totally inflexible with action or activity that does not agree with their plan. As you might suspect, successful planning and planners can be found somewhere in the middle of these two extremes.

I have spent a lot of time in my life helping people plan. I've worked with individuals who want to plan a better life, corporations who want to develop broad long-term strategic plans and everything in between. It has been my observation the following simple elements must exist in order for any plan to be successful:

1. A *reasonably* clear mental picture of the results you intend to accomplish.
2. A *reasonably* accurate assessment of the current situation and how it compares to the desired results.
3. An action plan with specific measurable steps to take you from where you are (Step 2 above) to where you desire to be (Step 1 above).
4. A *reasonable* amount of passion to achieve the desired results on the part of the person responsible for the plan.
5. A *fluid* commitment to the action plan on the part of the person(s) responsible for the plan.

To the hard-core planner, this formula will probably sound a little wishy-washy. What's all this talk about being "reasonable" and "fluid?" I use the word "reasonable" because that's all you can usually hope to know at the beginning of the planning process. Things *always* change as you learn more about a project and get farther into it. Change has a nasty habit of speeding up. For example, people used to have to physically stand in line at "the markets" in order to make a purchase. Now electrons often do it for us. It's called e-commerce. And electrons are speedy little things . . . they get in line in a hurry! In the old days (a few short years ago) you might have to camp out and stand in line to get a prize concert ticket. Now you may get the prize ticket if your modem is faster than the other person's modem . . . if your electrons beat their electrons to the market. If your five-year plan for getting tickets to the best concerts involves standing in line, you may have to be content listening to your wirehead friend's description of what it was like to be there!

Often plans fail because people try too hard to get everything crystal clear and perfect before they begin to execute a plan, or they try to follow the original plan to the letter when conditions have changed. It is preferable to have a reasonable idea of the results you desire to accomplish, to evaluate your current situation, and to develop a flexible action plan to accomplish the results.

Yes, you must have passion and commitment to accomplish anything. The stronger the passion the more likely you will succeed, but the commitment must absolutely exist and absolutely be fluid. Learn the value of fluidity from nature. Water running down a stream is not going to stop because there happens to be a rock in its path. Water is fluid and will simply find another way around the obstacle and continue on its merry way down the stream. Fluid commitments are entirely appropriate in carrying out and revising your own life plan. However, when you make a commitment to another person it should only be revised after discussion with and agreement with them.

Follow the five steps outlined in this chapter when you develop your next plan. If one of the steps is missing, the best you can probably hope for is frustration. In all likelihood, skipping one of these steps will lead to failure. For the leaders and managers among you, learn to ask questions and make observations to identify if these five elements exist in the plans that your teams bring to you. If one of these elements is missing, you may have what is referred to as a "teachable moment" in some circles. Take advantage of it and help your team get back on the path to success.

Develop sound plans; but *be reasonable* and maintain a *fluid commitment* to the success of your plan . . . a simple idea to make life better.

Quality

If the shoe fits, wear it!

For many years, I never paid too much attention to the kind of shoes I bought. I would buy name brand shoes and assume, within reason, shoes were shoes and I didn't need to spend too much time and effort on shoe selection. I was wrong!

During a business trip to Philadelphia, I was walking to my hotel in a light rain when I noticed that one foot felt soggy. I looked at the bottom of my shoe and sure enough, there was a hole in it. I was near a shopping mall, so I went to a nice shoe store, asked for the name-brand I was used to in my size, and expected to be out in a few minutes with my shoe problem solved. How-

Simple Works
87

ever, as I soon found out, my shoe purchase was not going to be so simple. For the first time in my life, I encountered a *professional* shoe salesperson.

He looked at my shoes and noticed some unusual wear patterns. He began asking me about my feet and how they felt after walking all day. He measured much more carefully than anyone had before. He talked to me a lot about my past experiences with shoes. After all of this, he went into the back of the store and brought out a pair of shoes that were a different size than I usually wore, and were also over twice as expensive as the shoes I usually bought. I was bracing to tell him to bring me the size and the price range that I requested. I slipped my feet into the shoes, he laced them up and I took them for a test walk around the store . . . and I had an honest to goodness, genuine, unexpected footwear epiphany! I couldn't believe how they felt. My feet were in heaven. I never would have imagined that different shoes could make such a difference. The shoe salesperson was my newest hero. I bought two pair.

For the next two weeks, I was amazed; the comfort was incredible and lasting. My feet, which I now realized had always bothered me and felt sore at the end of the day, were feeling better and better every day. I thought of all the years I had suffered for no reason. Why hadn't someone told me that high quality shoes could make such a difference in your life? And as for the fact that they were twice the price I had been paying . . . they lasted over four times longer. You do the math. I was suffering for no good reason and at the same time paying a higher real price for the lower quality, lower comfort shoes.

As you may have guessed by now, I quickly applied this lesson to other areas of my life, checking out where things just didn't fit as well as they should. I decided to end as many compromises as possible, and to spend the extra time, money or effort required to surround myself with things that "fit." I'm not suggesting that something twice as expensive is always better. I am suggesting that you take the time to find out what really fits your lifestyle and find a way to get it, regardless of the cost in time, money or effort. Look around for compromises, intentional and unintentional, and work out a plan to get rid of them. Examine your shoes, clothes, home, relationships and every aspect of your life and go for the "right fit." Surround yourself with quality *as you define it,* not as marketing experts, friends or other people define it. Look for the wear patterns in your life. What areas are showing more wear than they should and why? They may be telling you it is time to try on something new for size. Pay whatever price you must to get the highest quality you can in life. It's a simple idea to make life better.

Reading

What's in the Well
Comes Up in the Bucket!

The first time I heard the saying, "What's in the well comes up in the bucket," I thought how interesting it is that you could pack so much wisdom in so few simple words. I mean, "bucket" is probably the most complex word in the saying and it's not too hard for me to understand. It just makes common sense: If a well is full of water, and you dip a bucket in it and pull the bucket up, you can predict what will happen. It's unlikely that you are going to pull up a bucket full of milk, wine, beer, Dr. Pepper or Zima. You are most likely going to bring up . . . a bucket of water. That's true for water wells, and it's also true for mental "wells." Your mental well is what you draw on to create your life.

If you try to draw from an empty water well, your bucket will come up dry. That, too, is true of your life. Do you ever wonder why some people have so much to draw on to create opportunities and get them through the challenges that life presents to all of us?

One of the best ways I know to fill your mental well is reading. Years ago speaker and author Charlie "Tremendous" Jones wrote something I will never forget. He said, "You are the same today as you'll be in five years except for two things, the people you meet and the books you read." It sounds almost too simple to be profound, but following his advice can make a huge difference in your life.

Why? Just think about it: It may take an author ten, twenty or fifty years to accumulate enough knowledge to write a good book, but you can read the book and much of their knowledge can become yours in a matter of hours or days. What a great tool! So why not take advantage of others' experience, knowledge and understanding? By reading the words of people who are considered high achievers in a given field, you can significantly shorten your path to mastery. In addition to telling you how to be successful, authors often share the mistakes they made and the pitfalls they encountered.

Hopefully you can avoid making the same errors.

I have always been especially interested in reading about high achievers and trying to discover their secrets to success. I've found many have a passion for reading. Most were or are very busy people with many demands on their time . . . yet they find time to expand their minds by reading good books.

You can tap into this power, too. Pick great books to expand your knowledge in the following areas of your life:

- Family and personal relationships
- Intellectual development
- Spiritual development
- Career development
- Financial balance
- Health
- Recreational

Time spent reading good novels and pleasure books can also be just good fun. You can learn about other parts of the world, other cultures, and enrich your understanding of things you may never experience otherwise. If you are already a reader, think about the difference in your life because of the books you have read.

Let me give you an example of one of the most significant ways reading has shaped my life, taking me beyond my own narrow boundaries.

I was raised in the 50's and 60's in a small southern town. Like it or not, it was an environment of extreme racial prejudice. I often heard adults express attitudes about differences in race and characteristics of people who were different from my particular background. At the same time, I was very fortunate to have parents who would take me to the public library. (In a small town, this was one of our primary forms of entertainment!) Often on Sunday afternoon, we would go downtown, spend an hour or so at the library picking out our books for the week, and then go to the local ice cream parlor for a double dip of ice cream. Looking back, those were such joyous times in my life.

My first real taste of responsibility came from owning and using my library card. As we entered the doors to the library, I would always head straight to the children's section and load up on Dr. Seuss books. One book that I will never, never, ever forget was about Sneetches. Dr. Seuss wrote about the Star-Bellied Sneetches and Plain-Bellied Sneetches and Sylvester McMonkey McBean and his star belly machine. This book, which basically explained we are all the same inside, rescued me from the racist attitudes that were prevalent in my environment. It made it very clear to my young and impressionable mind that adults were not always right. It taught me I needed to look at other viewpoints and decide on my own what I thought was right. It taught me I could expand my current horizons by seeking great thoughts from great minds willing to share their knowledge with me through their books. I am eternally grateful that Dr. Seuss came into my life when he did to teach me these invaluable lessons.

Since then I have developed an insatiable appetite for reading. I have accepted the thoughts of authors who were uplifting and taught me things that resonated with my soul. I have rejected the theories of those who were sharing what I considered flawed logic, reasoning or emotions. In the end, I decide what makes sense to me, but I do it with information provided by some of the greatest minds in the universe by reading thoughts they felt important enough to share with the world. They have all helped me grow.

With books, I can always create a more level playing field for the game of life, because I have essentially the same access to great minds like Einstein or Edison or Ben Franklin or Freud or Jung as anyone else on the planet. Books allow me to meet people, go to places and have experiences that lift me above the place and time I just happen to physically be. Books ensure I am not the same person I was five years ago and that I will not be the same person five years from now. Books fill my well with wonderful contents and allow me to dip my bucket in a world much more wonderful than I ever imagined as a young person from a small corner of the world.

Expand your life through reading and you will open the doors to personal growth, joy and freedom from your physical environment. It's a simple idea to make life better.

Stumbling into Society's Traps

Stuck in the Web of Safety and Security

My friend John, a doctor, has often told me how difficult it was to make it through medical school and his
internship. For some of the medical students, everything seemed to come easy, but John struggled almost
every minute of every day. The good news was his parents were so proud of him. They beamed with joy as
they talked about "our son, the doctor." It seemed as
if all of their sentences began or ended with the state-
ment, "John is a doctor now, you know." For as long as
he could remember, they had wanted him to become a

doctor and had willingly made sacrifices to assure he would be able to achieve this goal.

John felt confident that the struggling would end when he finished his residency requirements and finally got out on his own as a practicing physician. The struggling continued. Then he thought, "If only I could get through this initial period of building my practice, things will be great. I can't wait until I am an established physician." The struggling continued. His practice did okay. The patients would come and go, the money would come and go . . . and the struggling continued to come and stay. The stress would come and stay, the headaches would come and stay, the frustration would come and stay . . . and the depression would come and stay.

Then late one night, while John sat in his office dealing with the huge stack of paperwork that seemed to show up each day, he had a sudden flash of insight. Why hadn't he thought of this sooner? How did he get so far down this path without realizing it? *He didn't like being a doctor! He never liked it and he never would.*

No wonder it was so difficult for him. He had friends who loved medicine. Medicine was their life's passion. That's why it was so easy for them. But he had invested over twenty years of his life in something that provided him with no joy, no fulfillment and no satisfaction. He wondered, "What can I do about it now? I'm in debt for this building. I'm in debt for all of the equipment in this office. I'm in debt for the huge doctor's house that I bought. I'm in debt for the expensive doctor's car that I drive. And my parents get such joy out of talking about, "our son, the doctor." Being a doctor is all I really know how to do."

John finished his paperwork and went home. The next day he went back to work and the struggle continued. The next day he went back to work . . . and the next day . . . and the next day . . . and the next day. John and the office copy machine, that he still owed $1,200 on, had much in common. They continued to do the same thing over and over and over, with no passion and no joy. But now they no longer have this in common . . . one day the copy machine finally broke down.

How many people do you know like John? How many people do you know who are in a trap, clinging to the illusion of safety and security because that's what everybody expects them to do or, that's all they know how to do?

Our life's work should be our *life's calling*. Our calling, in turn, should be driven by a strong inner urge or impulse that summons us to follow a certain path in life. Certainly most of us are not called to be doctors. However, the most important thing about John's story is that

John was not called to be a doctor. John had stumbled onto a path that was important to his parents. It was probably important to all of his teachers. It was probably important to all of his friends. Later on it was certainly important to all of his creditors. But being a doctor was not John's calling. The farther along this path John traveled, the more society expected him to stay on his chosen path.

What happened to John can, and does, happen to many of us. The world is full of doctors, business people, factory workers, salespeople, stay at home parents and others who have stumbled onto the wrong path in life. Many can't hear, or sense, their calling because they never slow down and listen for it or think about it. They just get caught up in the whirlwind of life and end up doing what everybody else thinks they are supposed to do. In even worse shape, are those people who hear their calling and ignore it. Their passions, gifts and talents are calling them to go in one direction, but they are too invested in another direction that offers the illusion of safety and security.

Here's the good news. For most of us, it is not too late to listen for, discover and follow our true calling in life. All you have to do is make new choices. They may be small, seemingly insignificant choices that gently send you in a new direction, or they may be bold, radical choices that derail your current life and place you on an entirely new set of tracks.

Could there be some pain involved when you make new life choices? It is certainly a possibility. But if you're in a trap, aren't you already in pain? Life is sometimes like a toothache. You may suffer a dull, throbbing, continuous nagging pain for a long time. Maybe the pain is annoying, but it is not severe enough to take any radical action. So you may rub some pain reliever on it or avoid using it and you put up with the pain. Eventually you have had enough and you go and get it pulled. This may result in a much higher level of pain in the present moment, but it also marks the beginning of true relief. Soon the throbbing and nagging pain are gone for good. You wonder why you didn't take action sooner. The pain was worth it.

Do you know your true calling in life? Have you taken the time to think about it and explore the possibilities? Are you aware of your calling and ignoring it? Is your life like a big, dull, annoying toothache? Don't exchange another 86,400 seconds of your life for someone else's idea of what is right for you. If you have been doing this for a long time, find a place right now to sit quietly, allow your mind to be still and listen for your calling. Stop clinging to other people's ideas about the life you should be leading. Escape from society's trap of expectations. Take some little steps or take some big steps and begin your new journey today. Begin living the life you were truly meant to live . . . it's a simple idea to make life better.

Taking Things Personally

Iceberg Dramas

At some point you've undoubtedly felt unjustly at-
tacked by someone: a customer service rep at a bank, a
friend or relative, your boss or co-worker, the guy at the
drive-through window or a client. Sad to say, people are
sometimes out of sorts, and the people around them
bear the brunt of it. It's no fun to be on the receiving
end of someone's anger, or mistreatment, or failure to
respond in a positive way. But I'm going to suggest
something: Don't take it personally.

Life is like an iceberg drama. All you can normally observe in other people's lives is the tip of the iceberg; most of the real drama is going on under the surface. Most of the time, it's the hidden drama that causes others to respond to us inappropriately. When someone has a surly attitude, it might be because of something that happened at home. Perhaps a child is sick, or a relative just died, or they can't make ends meet. Perhaps that person is worrying about losing a job in a corporate layoff, or waiting for the report from their last doctor's visit. Maybe they just found out their spouse is cheating on them, or it could be that their teenager is flunking out of school. We all have difficult times in our lives, and we don't always go about broadcasting them. People may not know there's something serious, or even just scary, going on behind the scenes.

The point is, people's negative reactions usually have absolutely nothing to do with what's happening right now, and everything to do with their own insecurities or problems. Therefore, another persons actions and reactions have nothing to do with us. *So why take it personally?*

It's true in the service we receive, it's true in our business relationships, and it's true in our personal lives. People yell at their kids when they're really upset with their spouse. They argue with their spouse when they're upset with their boss. They treat their friends poorly when they're really upset with themselves.

How much mental anguish, frustration, stress and negativity could you eliminate from your life if you learned to *not take things personally?*

Here's an example of a radical way to react to negativity. Suppose you arrive at work one day and one of your co-workers has left you a particularly terse voicemail. Ask yourself, "I wonder why she did that. Could something be bothering her that I don't know about?" Rather than dash off a defensive email, or storm into her office to rebut her attack, be kind. Smile. Ask about her day. You will do more to change a bad situation through this unexpected act of kindness than you will ever get by counter attacking her.

How many times have you been sitting in slow traffic and watched as some inconsiderate driver bullied ahead, raced down the expressway in the emergency lane to get ahead of everyone else, or have been put in jeopardy by someone going sixty miles an hour who cuts in front of you and then slams on their brakes? What's your initial reaction, anger? How would your feelings be different if you knew their child had just been seriously injured in a school bus accident and lay at death's door? Would that change how you felt about their actions?

If you want to change the world, do it by reacting with understanding rather than anger or retaliation. You can best teach people a lesson by not trying to "teach them a lesson."

What would your life be like if you learned to never take anything personally? What would you be giving up and what would you gain? As you encounter people who give you a hard time, ask yourself what you can learn from the experience. Examine your own life and try to think of a time when you were guilty of the same type of behavior. Was there something upsetting you, or causing you to lash out? Try to imagine that something similar may be happening in that person's life that could make them less than patient.

Regardless of whether someone's behavior or attack on you has any basis in fact, there is no value in taking anything personally. Reacting to other people's attacks is like turning over control of your life and your feelings to them. For example, the other day, I was at a red light, and the guy behind me was really angry, making gestures, yelling. At first, I started to let it get to me. Then I realized that it had nothing to do with me. So, I had a choice: I could take it personally, feel angry, go to work and recount the story about the jerk in traffic, and carry those negative feelings around all morning. Or I could realize it had nothing to do with me and have a nice, pleasant day. Thank goodness I saw that the choice was mine, and I felt good about not filling my day with negativity. Who was in control of my day, the driver I didn't even know, or me?

Reacting to another person's misery is like taking on their problems and making them yours. If I take on your problems, and I get mad, then I take my anger out on someone else, and now my relationship with them is jeopardized. Then they get upset, yell at someone in their circle, and so on. Someone along the line needs to stop the negative locomotive from building steam . . . could it be you?

We're all in this life together, all trying to get the most out of life. Sometimes our struggle affects other people in a negative way. You may never know what's happening to cause another person to act the way they do. But you can give them the benefit of the doubt. Start today and make the choice to never take anything personally . . . it's a simple idea to make life better.

Uniformity

Preventing Middle Life Crisis

Most of the time the word "uniformity" is not very appealing to me. It conjures up images of being just like everyone else, staying in a straight line, being ordinary and average. But that's not the kind of uniformity that I am talking about in this chapter. I am talking about developing more uniformity between the "person" who is inside you and the "person" the outside world sees when they interact with you. Usually, these two "people" are about as alike as Danny DeVito and Arnold Schwarzenegger were in the movie *Twins*.

Isn't it great that as people get older they seem to care less about what others think of them, spending less time trying to please people and more time doing what they want to do? They live an outer life that is more uniform with their inner desires and feelings. And isn't it ironic that this is also the way kids live their lives. Very young children spontaneously say what's on their minds and do what they feel like doing. Too bad that somewhere between youth and old age our inner life gets out of sync with our outer life. We often lose the uniformity between what we internally desire and how we outwardly live.

Years ago, when my children were very young, I gave a speech at a town about 100 miles from where I lived. Since it was a short trip and I was going to drive, my wife and children went with me. After the speech, we got away later than I thought and I knew we wouldn't get back home until about midnight. I was very tired and very ready to get home and go to bed. But accomplishing this goal would not be so easy on this night.

At the time, we lived in an apartment complex that had a pool and a hot tub. My children absolutely loved to sit in the hot tub. It was one of those "family bonding" things we did a lot. When we got in the car, the kids asked if we could spend some time in the hot tub when we got home. I was tired, so I did what most parents would do in this situation. I said, "No." Not only did I say no, I thought to myself . . . I am raising crazy children. Unfortunately, the kids had actually listened to my speech, during which I had pontificated about being spontaneous and learning how to put some of the fun back into your life. Clearly, I was trapped. I started thinking about how to convince the kids that a midnight dip was a bad idea . . . that it was too late, that we needed to get in bed, that we would do it at a more appropriate time. And then I realized something momentous: I was wrong and they were right. I realized that if I were their age, I would think that going in the hot tub at midnight was a fabulous idea. I realized I had just given a speech telling people to do things exactly like what my children were proposing. So, I said, "Yes. Let's do it." The night sky was beautiful, the warm jets of water were relaxing and the time with my family was special. All in all, it was a night we will never forget.

We seem to lose uniformity between our inner desires and our outer life for several reasons. We forget to have fun. We try too hard to please others. We try too hard to be what others think we should be. In my own case, I spent the first six years of my career being what "the marketplace" wanted me to be.

During college I decided that I wanted to be a CPA. Looking back, it was such a ridiculous notion. I know exactly why I chose this goal and it had nothing to do with my inner desires or talents. It had everything to do with the desires of the job market at the time. People with accounting degrees were getting jobs at good salaries. That sounded like a good plan, so I got the degree, became a CPA, and was on an accelerated path to success in the business. I was also very unfulfilled. After investing over six years in a career, suddenly I was stumped. I couldn't understand, with everything going so well (according to everyone else), why I was so restless? I was out running one day when the answer came to me . . . I didn't like being a CPA. I didn't like the work, and it wasn't even close to what I really wanted to do with my life. It was as simple as that. I got into it for the wrong reasons and it was time to get out. I should have known something was amiss a few years earlier when I had a personality profile evaluation for a training class that I attended. The instructor came up to me during one of the breaks and jokingly accused me of lying on my class registration form. She said, based on my personality profile, it was virtually impossible for me to be a CPA. My profile didn't fit whatever a CPA was supposed to be like. Ultimately, letting go of "being a CPA" felt great. I reinvented myself and changed careers within a month.

Marriages often get started in a similar way. It seems like the right thing to do at the time. Other people your age are all starting to get married. One party starts the marriage snowball rolling down the hill and the other party (who may not quite be ready) doesn't stop it.

There arc two things you can do to keep some uniformity between your inside desires and outer life.

1. Take the time to *know* the "beat of your own drum." If you're not aware of it, you can't march to it.
2. March to the beat of your own drum, no matter how loudly other people try to beat on their drum.

Thank goodness *it's never too late.* You may not be able to make the transition overnight, or without discomfort and fear. It may be very difficult to let go of your "investment" in a job, or in a relationship. It may be difficult to keep from conforming to what society expects of an adult between youth and old age. You may not be able to go back to the crazy, fun-loving, midnight dipping days of your youth, but you can get a head start on one of the best parts of getting old. You can start doing what you want to do and caring less about what other people think about it. You can bring more uniformity into your inner and outer life. It's a simple idea to make life better.

Vocabulary

Words of Wisdom

Phrases come into and go out of vogue, and some are harmless. I remember when "groovy" was the word of choice to describe something desirable. Lately the phrase I seem to hear most, especially in restaurants, is "No problem." When someone does something for you, and you say, "Thanks," they say "No problem." It's become a substitute for "You're welcome." Something about that seems backwards. Saying "no problem" puts the emphasis on the server's convenience, as if the customer has asked for something he or she wasn't entitled to, and that the server has responded out of the kindness of his heart.

No doubt you've also heard, "Don't mention it," as if in this day and age we don't need small niceties. Wouldn't you rather hear, "I'm happy to do it" or "My pleasure?" Those phrases seem so much more positive. Perhaps they sound hokey, but as fast as we're all moving, and as hard as our world has become, we could all use a little tender loving care in the form of gentleness of manner.

Another sort of double negative I hear is, "I don't disagree with that." What would be wrong with saying, "I agree with you." It says the same thing; yet, it's a positive way to express your belief, and it validates the other person's idea.

So what does all this vocabulary stuff have to do with creating a better life? Words have an impact on what we believe about ourselves and about others. A friend of mine is a very bright and beautiful woman, and her sister is equally bright and beautiful. When they were children, their parents told them, "Kris is the smart one, and Jan is the pretty one." No surprise here: Kris grew up to think of herself as beautiful, and she didn't have very high expectations of herself when it came to intellectual pursuits. She felt like she could never measure up. Jan, on the other hand, saw herself as intelligent, but never felt good about her appearance. Although she is a beautiful woman, she's been working at trying to be attractive all her life. Kris' and Jan's parents shaped their lives by a simple choice of words.

Now I'm going to admit something a bit embarrassing. When I was a teenager, I had a Troy Donohue-Sandra Dee scrapbook. You may never have heard of these two actors, but in the 1960s, they were BIG. Despite my love for them (especially Troy), I never wrote a fan letter. I've since traded in my teenage infatuation with movie stars for admiration of authors. About three years ago, I read a book by Patricia T. O'Conner called *Woe Is I,* and it blew me away. It is, believe it or not, a grammar book; nevertheless, it is as entertaining as any book I've ever read. Guess what I did? I wrote her a fan letter. Ms. O'Conner has several best-selling books, and I never dreamed of hearing one word back from her. She could have ignored my letter, which I halfway expected. She could have even sent me back a form letter (a sure way to let someone know how utterly unimportant they are). But several weeks later, I received a *handwritten* card from THE Patricia T. O'Conner. Informal, down to earth, it even included the words, "blah, blah, blah," which I loved! She even complimented my writing style. I'm sure Ms. O'Conner has long since forgotten the three sentences she jotted on that card. I never will. At times when I've doubted whether I could write books, I've thought of her card. It may have taken her two minutes to write that note, but its affect on me will last a lifetime.

You don't have to be a famous author to give people encouragement. We all have a chance every day to choose our words, and to build people up or tear them down. Anytime you give guidance, do you just focus on the things people do wrong, and tell them how to fix them, or do you take equal time to praise the things they do right? Or, do you always tag a negative onto a positive, such as: "Great job, but . . ." A friend of mine says that whenever someone says the word "but" you can forget whatever they've said up to that point; whatever comes *after* the "but" is what the person really thinks!

Try this experiment. Begin listening to yourself and to others, and noticing how often negative words or sentiments appear. I think you'll be surprised at how often it happens. Now here's the challenge: Anytime you begin to say something in a negative way, stop yourself and rephrase it to be positive. The results will be amazing.

A good place to start practicing positive talk is with yourself. Have you ever seen someone make a mistake and then say, "Oh, I'm so stupid." Or, "What an idiot." Saying such harsh things is like beating yourself up emotionally, using words to berate and abuse yourself. Instead, what would happen if you were more accepting of yourself, kinder and more considerate of your own feelings? Strangely enough, if you can begin with saying nice things to yourself, showing tolerance and acceptance, you will find that you magically become more tolerant and accepting of others.

What if each of us focused on adding just one positive phrase to our vocabulary, or eliminating one negative? What if you said, "I'm happy to do it," instead of "No problem?" Send an email to a friend with a compliment or reminder of how important that person is to you. Ask a friend how he's doing. Tell someone what an impact they've had on your life.

Practice saying everything in a positive way instead of a negative one, and see what happens. Could you affect the reality of our world? Could you contribute to making things more positive in your life and in the lives of people around you? Wouldn't that be groovy? Try it and see . . . it's a simple idea to make life better.

World-Changing

There's No Place Like Home

World-changing is a fairly common goal among human beings, and I personally think being thought of as a world-changer would be pretty cool. When people asked me what I do, I could say, "I write books, watch some TV, play guitar, change the world, play golf, and raise children." Yes, I think being a W. C. (world-changer) has a good ring to it.

As cool as it might be, world-changing sounds like a pretty big task. I do have one idea that I think makes world-changing simpler. It is:

Change yourself before you even think about trying to change someone else.

The primary benefit from starting with *your world* and *yourself* is that you can actually change these things. You know how difficult at times it is to change things you *can* control, so why not stick with these things and quit trying to change things you *cannot* control?

Can you change someone else? Changing is a very personal choice. No one else can make the decision to change for you, and you cannot make the decision to change for others. In the end, every individual on the face of the planet must decide what he or she is going to do about a suggested (or ordered) change.

If you study history you know that a lot of people have been ordered to change by some fairly impressive and influential people . . . like kings and queens. And quite a few have weighed the consequences of not changing (like beheading) with the pain of changing. Many changed. But others decided to accept pain, grief and even death rather than change. Patrick Henry is most famous for illustrating this concept in a speech to the Virginia Provincial Convention in 1775:

"I know not what course others may take; but as for me, give me liberty or give me death!

Lucky for Patrick, it turned out to be liberty.

Can you help someone else change? Perhaps, but probably not in the way you might think; not by focusing on teaching them, but merely by living the changes you choose. That old saw, "Actions speak louder than words," is a very accurate theory. You influence others most by your actions, the choices you make and the changes you accept in your life. Therein lies the secret to world-changing. If the change you desire is worthwhile, others will see the positive effects of the change in *your life* and want to join the club.

How do you eat an elephant? You take one bite at a time. How do you change the world? You deal with one person at a time. And that person is you. Be the change you want to see in the world and watch it spread among the other people in your circle of influence. It's a simple idea to make life better.

"X" Marks the Spot

Being Right Here, Right Now

When you are lost, three of the most reassuring words you can see on a map or diagram are, "You are here." You may be on a trip in the car, looking for a store at the mall, hiking on a trail in the woods, trying to find your way around a huge resort hotel or hospital. Suddenly you realize that you do not have a clue as to where you are in relation to where you desire to be. Then you come upon a directional marker with an "X" marking the spot where you stand. What a relief! You can study the map for a moment, quickly become reoriented and determine how you will be able to get from where you are to where you want to be. You are back on the path that you desire.

Years ago, I went on a retreat out West to learn about the Native American culture including the medicine wheel, planting and hunting traditions and other spiritual beliefs and customs. Our guide appeared to be an extraordinary person. It's difficult to express exactly what it was about him that was unique, but he was "different" from anyone I had ever met before. Our group was made up of "successful" people with a reasonably good supply of money, titles, possessions and egos. Our guide seemed to have none of these. Oddly enough, however, he didn't seem to have any interest in the things we had, but we all were intensely interested in having what he had: peace, serenity, confidence and true success as a human being. We had "store-bought" success; he seemed to have the real, homemade thing. The best way I can describe it is to say that I had that feeling you get when you are lost and you first see the "You are here" X on the map. This guy had his own internal "X" that seemed to move around with him. He was always oriented, in the present and on the right path.

One afternoon, we went to a certain spot on the top of a mountain, and someone asked him, "Why are we here?" He ignored the real intent of the person's question, turned to all of us and said:

"At this moment, you are the sole reason for your ancestors' existence."

Our guide then told us several stories about buffalos, rock people, hawks and other flying creatures. The stories were fascinating and they all supported one belief . . . live your life as if you are always where "X-Marks the Spot." Draw an imaginary circle around your spot, and stay inside that circle as much as you can. Don't worry about the distant past or the distant future. They're too far away from the spot where you are right now. Keep the distant culprits out of the circle as much as you can. *Try to stay oriented in the present*—let your "X" move with you wherever you go.

I believe, as our guide said, that I am the sole reason, at this time, for my ancestors' existence. I believe that you are the sole reason, at this time, for your ancestors' existence. On the map of your ancestry, you are sitting right on top of the "X." You have the potential to influence the family of mankind by your actions today. We have already said it several different ways in this book: Be here . . . be present physically, mentally, emotionally and spiritually.

We often spend too much of our lives either trying to physically or mentally get "from here to there." Why not spend more time just being here, where "X-Marks the Spot" for you? Learn to spend time relaxing into joyful participation in life as it unfolds . . . it's a simple idea to make life better.

Yellow Flowers

Nothing Clashes in a Garden

As the so-called "baby boomers" age, an awful lot of us are now grandparents. What a relief. We can feed our grandchildren ice cream for dinner and not worry for one minute about whether they are poorly nourished or that we are spoiling the kids.

I think a good bit of the joy of grandparenting lies in what we're learning about ourselves rather than what we're learning about those beautiful 3-year-olds.

I have learned a lot from the experience. For instance, when I was younger, I didn't have the patience to garden. Developing a beautiful garden takes several years, and as the plants mature, the picture changes in size, shape and color. There's no way to know exactly what the garden will look like next year, what will die or what will flourish.

When I was totally focused on my career, and trying to raise my child, I never had the time or the patience for the gardener's waiting game. But as my life has become more serene, I've developed a taste for things that take a little time to blossom. The luscious surprise is worth the wait.

I discovered this a few years ago when I put in a perennial garden. When I was choosing what to put in, I selected flowers that were all the colors I love: purple, fuchsia, pink, white. My garden advisor also recommended I include some things she knew would be hearty and round out the landscape. One of those was black-eyed Susans, a tall, golden flower that I don't particularly care for. Oh well, I thought, she's the expert.

The next spring, I watched as the flowers started to bloom, and sure enough, the black-eyed Susans practically took over a bed. They were bright and cheerful, and indeed, able to withstand just about any sort of weather (or gardener) abuse. Everyone said they were handsome, but I just never really liked them much.

Then, just a year or so after we planted the garden, my grandson, Gabriel, was born. He was just about 15 months old when I took him out for his first garden adventure. I pointed out my favorites—all the pinks and purples—as well as the worms, and assorted bugs. What did he like best? The black-eyed Susans, of course. That's where the butterflies and honeybees congregate. Each time we went out for our garden perusal, he headed straight for "the yellow flowers."

To this day, yellow is his favorite color. And I must admit I've gotten to like it myself.

Yellow flowers represent the myriad of beautiful, bright spots in our lives that we can't overlook. They're the source of unexpected joys that come from being open to new experiences.

Everyone needs to try some yellow flowers. They may not be your favorites at first, and they may not be what you'd select, but sometimes our greatest joys come from the things that are put in front of us that we don't ask for.

You don't have to wait to become a grandparent to discover this. Add some yellow flowers to your life . . . it's a simple idea that makes life better.

Zen and the Art of Airports

The Fable of the Rental Car Agent and the Executive

Do you think it's possible that any human being could be a frequent traveler and remain serene, given all the things that happen to disrupt travel plans?

A friend told me a story of how her sister, a business executive, had an important business meeting, and had arranged for a particular rental car that was vital to her trip's success. It had something to do with being able to fit all the important people in one vehicle. The executive had double-checked the arrangements prior to her arrival, and was assured all was in readiness. When she got to the car agency, however, the rental agent informed her the car was not available. Worst of all, the agent was totally blasé, apparently not concerned one bit for the woman's inconvenience.

The executive's blood pressure went off the charts. She informed the agent of her important meeting, about having double-checked the reservation and about the obvious incompetence of the company in having screwed things up. Ranting and raving for three or four minutes, she impugned the integrity of everyone in sight, and made it perfectly clear how important she was and how this would affect everyone.

The car rental agent, who had practically filed her nails throughout the tirade, spoke up. She said, "Lady, at the end of my shift, I'm going home to be with my kids, to cook them dinner and read them a story. While I do that, I will not be thinking about you, your car, or this incident. You can scream all you want, but it's not going to ruin my day. It's only going to ruin yours."

Well, now, there's a revelation. The tirade was more painful to the giver than the receiver.

There's no excuse for insensitive service, but in the

hectic world of travel, can you avoid such incidents? It's not likely. Just as it's not likely you'll control the many other areas of your life where mishaps can occur.

An unavailable rental car, a cancelled flight, late arrival, or lost bag are not exactly the stuff that great trips are made of. But once things are set in motion, what are your choices? Get upset, spend the day recounting the tragedy and spread anger to all of those around. Or, calmly accept the situation and find a way to still enjoy the day.

Inconveniences are a matter of course, not only in travel, but in our daily lives. These inconveniences are generally outside our control. But the degree to which we let them affect us is totally within our control. A small detour is just that—small—and we don't have to make it a catastrophe. Where is the catastrophe, anyway? It's all in our heads, just like our serenity. What people do around us doesn't disturb us, what disturbs us is how we react.

Take the "bad" things that happen to you in a day and shrink them down to size. Don't give them room in your head to create chaos or dissatisfaction. Deal with them as tiny speed bumps and go on. Just a simple idea to make life better.

Simple Works

Parting Thoughts

Throughout this book we have tried to keep things simple. We believe there is no need to change that strategy now. If you liked an idea that you read about in this book, give it a try. It's simple; a sound idea will help you more if you act on it rather than just reading and talking about it. There is often a fine line between teaching and preaching. Our intention in writing this book is to share and teach. If at any time it sounded as if we were preaching, we humbly admit that we are *"Simple Works* sinners." As authors, we write about many good ideas that we are still trying to turn into habits in our own lives; so we will be hanging in there with you, just trying to do a little better everyday.

We encourage you to read the book several times. Something that didn't resonate with you the first time may make more sense as your life circumstances change. We also encourage you to share copies of the book with your friends. Treat *Simple Works* like a big, fat greeting card and send messages to your friends by marking certain chapters. Spouses can send books with chapter "D" marked. If you and a friend have had an argument, send them a copy with chapter "F" marked. If you know someone who is going through a disaster, send him or her a copy with chapter "H" marked. Send your Mom or Grandmother a copy of chapter "M", a bag of popcorn and tell her you will be right over for a fun snack. Say it simply, say it with *Simple Works*.

To keep things simple for us, we randomly picked the alphabet and wrote about one topic for each letter. One person who read a first draft of the book and didn't notice the alphabet pattern said, "Hey, this is pretty cool! You designed the book so you could focus on one idea every two weeks." After hearing this, we thought . . . hey, that sounds like a simple idea to make life better.

Thank you for choosing to share some time with us. We are honored to be able to share some ideas with you and hope our paths will continue to cross in life.

About the Authors

Chris Crouch, author, trainer and speaker, is President of DME Training and Consulting. His training focuses on helping people significantly improve their personal productivity and career satisfaction. His career reflects impressive success in both the financial services industry and personal success training. In addition to *Simple Works*, he is co-author of *The Contented Achiever*. He lives in Memphis, Tennessee and can be reached at CCSeagull888@aol.com.

Susan M. Drake is the founder of Spellbinders, Inc., a 15-year-old marketing and communications consulting company. Susan enjoys helping her clients use a variety of media to talk to all the people who are important to their success. She lives in Memphis, Tennessee, with her husband and three cats, and within walking distance of her daughter and two grandchildren (all of whom contribute to making her life happier, but not necessarily simpler!) She can be reached at sdrake@midsouth.rr.com.

Consumer Order

Payable in US funds only. Book price $15.95 each copy. Postage & handling: US/Can. $3.25 for one book, $1.50 for each additional book. International: $6.50 for one book, $3.00 for each additional. We accept Visa, MC, AMEX, checks ($15.00 fee for returned checks) and money orders. No Cash/ COD. Call 866-222-0028 or 901-748-2142, fax 901-748-1994, or mail your orders to:

Black Pants Publishing

3410 S. Tournament Dr.

Memphis, TN 38125

Bill my credit card:

cc# _____ exp. _____

_____ Visa _____ MC _____ AMEX

Signature_____

Please ship _____ copies of *Simple Works*.

Bill to: _____	Book total:_____
Address:_____	Applicable
City_____ST:_____ ZIP:_____	Sales Tax: _____
Daytime phone #_____	Postage &
Ship to:_____	Handling: _____
Address:_____	Total Amt.
City_____ST:_____ ZIP:_____	Due:_____

Please add 8.25% sales tax for books shipped to Tennessee addresses.

Simple Works is available at special quantity discounts for sales promotions, premiums, fund-raising, or educational use. Special books or book excerpts can also be created to fit specific needs.

Call toll-free at 866-222-0028, email to *info@blackpantspublishing.com* or write to:

Black Pants Publishing

3410 S. Tournament Dr.

Memphis, TN 38125